THE LONDONERS GUIDE TO GETTING RICH

Forget Mayfair, the New Rich are Bossing Online

Genevieve Velzian

Copyright © 2024 Genevieve Velzian

All rights reserved

All recommendations and opinion's are the author's own and they do not replace seeking your own legal advice. The author accepts no liability.

No part of this book may be reproduced, or stored in a retrieval system, or transmitted in any form or by any means, electronic, mechanical, photocopying, recording, or otherwise, without express written permission of the publisher.

CONTENTS

Copyright 3
Introduction 3
Understanding Wealth 3
Navigating London's Financial Landscape 3
Entrepreneurship in London 3
Where to Invest in London Property 3
Investing Wisely 3
Employment Strategies 3
Side Hustles 3
50 Ways to Make Money Online 3
Financial Management 3
Leveraging Technology 3
Save Some Cash 3
Networking and Mentorship 3
Living Like a Millionaire in London 3
Maintaining a Balanced Life 3
Who's Already Winning? 3
Navigating Economic Cycles 3
Continuous Learning and Personal Development 3
Conclusion 3
The End 3
About The Author 3
Title Page 1

INTRODUCTION

Welcome to "A Londoner's Guide to Getting Rich," a comprehensive manual designed to help you navigate the financial opportunities and challenges unique to our vibrant city.

London, with its bustling financial district, world-class educational institutions, and diverse job market, offers unparalleled opportunities for wealth creation. However, the high cost of living, competitive environment, and complex financial landscape can make the journey to financial success seem daunting.

This book aims to demystify the process, providing you with practical advice, proven strategies, and real-life examples to help you achieve your financial goals.

Purpose of the Book

The purpose of this book is simple: to equip you with the knowledge and tools necessary to build and sustain wealth in London. Whether you are a young professional starting your career, an entrepreneur with big ambitions, or someone looking to make smart investments, this guide is tailored to your needs.

We will cover a wide range of topics, from managing your finances and making wise investment choices to leveraging technology and maintaining a balanced life. By the end of this book, you will have a clear roadmap to financial success, tailored specifically to the unique opportunities and challenges of living in London.

My Story

Allow me to share a bit of my own journey. When I first moved to London, I was overwhelmed by the sheer scale and pace of the city. The high cost of living, the competitive job market, and the seemingly endless opportunities made it difficult to know where to start. I started out in marketing, before realising that data was my true passion.

Through perseverance, financial planning, and leveraging the resources available, I was able to navigate these challenges and build a successful and fulfilling life. I have several properties, several businesses, and my husband and I started a sports supplement business that is now worth in the millions.

My experiences, both the successes and the lessons learned from failures, form the foundation of this book. I hope that by sharing my story, I can inspire and guide you on your own path to financial success in this incredible city.

Structure of the Book

This book is divided into ten chapters, each focusing on a different aspect of wealth creation. We begin by understanding what wealth means and the importance of having the right mindset.

From there, we delve into practical strategies for navigating London's financial landscape, securing high-paying jobs, starting and growing businesses, making wise investments, and much more. Each chapter is filled with practical advice, actionable steps, and real-life examples to help you apply what you learn to your own life.

Final Thoughts

London is a city of dreams and opportunities. While the path to wealth may be challenging, it is certainly attainable with the right knowledge and strategies. This book is your guide to unlocking the potential that London offers, helping you to not only achieve financial success but also to live a balanced and fulfilling life. I invite you to embark on this journey with me, armed with the insights and tools that have helped many others, including myself, to get rich in London.

Welcome to "A Londoner's Guide to Getting Rich." Let's get started on your path to financial success.

UNDERSTANDING WEALTH

Defining Wealth

When we talk about wealth, it's essential to understand that it means different things to different people. In the context of this book, wealth isn't just about having a vast amount of money in the bank.

Instead, it's about achieving financial security, having the freedom to make choices that improve your quality of life, and creating opportunities for yourself and your family. In London, a city known for its high living costs and diverse economic landscape, understanding what wealth means to you personally is the first step towards achieving it.

Wealth in London can encompass owning property in a desirable area, having a robust investment portfolio, or running a successful business. It might also mean having the financial flexibility to travel, pursue hobbies, or provide for your family without stress. By defining what wealth means to you, you can set clear, personalised goals that will guide your financial journey.

Mindset Matters

The journey to wealth begins with the right mindset. A positive, growth-oriented mindset can significantly influence your ability to achieve financial success. This involves believing that you can improve your financial situation, being open to learning and adapting, and maintaining resilience in the face of challenges.

In London, where the cost of living is high and the competition can be fierce, having a growth mindset is crucial. It allows you to see opportunities where others see obstacles and to keep pushing forward even when the going gets tough. Cultivating such a mindset involves self-reflection, continuous learning, and surrounding yourself with supportive and like-minded individuals.

Consider adopting these strategies to develop a growth mindset:

Embrace Challenges: See obstacles as opportunities to learn and grow rather than as setbacks.

Learn from Criticism: Use constructive feedback as a tool for improvement.

Celebrate Successes: Acknowledge your achievements, no matter how small, to build confidence and momentum.

Stay Persistent: Keep pushing forward, even when progress seems slow.

Setting Goals

Once you've defined what wealth means to you and have adopted a growth mindset, the next step is to set realistic and achievable financial goals. Clear goals provide direction and motivation, helping you stay focused on your path to wealth.

Effective goal-setting involves:

Specificity: Define your goals in precise terms. For example, rather than saying "I want to save money," specify "I want to save £10,000 in the next year."

Measurability: Ensure that you can track your progress. This could involve setting milestones or regular check-ins to assess how you're doing.

Achievability: Set goals that are challenging but attainable. Unrealistic goals can lead to frustration and discouragement.

Relevance: Make sure your goals align with your broader financial aspirations and personal values.

Time-bound: Establish a clear timeline for achieving your goals, which creates a sense of urgency and keeps you accountable.

Let's take an example. Suppose you aim to buy a property in London. Your goal might be: "I want to save £50,000 for a deposit on a flat in Zone 2 within the next five years." This goal is specific (saving £50,000 for a deposit), measurable (you can track your savings), achievable (with a well-structured savings plan), relevant (aligning with your desire to own property), and time-bound (five-year timeline).

Actionable Steps

Assess Your Current Situation: Before setting your goals, take a close look at your current financial situation. This includes your income, expenses, debts, and savings. Understanding where you stand will help you set realistic goals and create a plan to achieve them.

Create a Financial Plan: Develop a comprehensive financial plan that outlines how you will achieve your goals. This plan should include your income sources, savings strategy, investment plans, and any steps you need to take to reduce debt.

Monitor and Adjust: Regularly review your progress towards your goals and make adjustments as needed. Life is unpredictable, and your financial plan should be flexible enough to accommodate changes in your circumstances or priorities.

Seek Professional Advice: Consider consulting a financial advisor to help you create and implement your financial plan. An advisor can provide valuable insights, help you avoid common pitfalls, and keep you on track.

Conclusion

Understanding wealth is the foundational step in your journey to financial success in London. By defining what wealth means to you, adopting a growth mindset, and setting clear, achievable goals, you lay the groundwork for a prosperous future.

Remember, wealth isn't just about the money you accumulate but about creating a life that offers security, freedom, and fulfilment. As you progress through this book, you'll gain the knowledge and tools to turn your financial aspirations into reality, one step at a time.

NAVIGATING LONDON'S FINANCIAL LANDSCAPE

Cost of Living

Living in London comes with its own set of financial challenges, primarily driven by the high cost of living. Understanding these expenses is crucial to managing your finances effectively and making informed decisions.

Housing: Rent or mortgage payments will likely be your most significant expense. London property prices are among the highest in the world, and rental rates vary widely depending on the area. Central locations like Westminster and Kensington command premium prices, while outer boroughs like Croydon or Barking and Dagenham offer more affordable options.

Utilities and Council Tax: In addition to rent or mortgage payments, you must account for utilities such as electricity, gas, water, and internet. Council tax, which varies based on the borough and property value, is another significant expense.

Transport: London has an extensive public transport network, but costs can add up. Consider purchasing a Travelcard or using an Oyster card to manage expenses. Cycling or walking can be cost-effective alternatives for shorter journeys.

Food and Dining: Groceries and dining out can be expensive in London. Shopping at local markets, using discount supermarkets, and cooking at home can help reduce costs. Dining out in less touristy areas or taking advantage of restaurant deals can also save money.

Entertainment and Leisure: London offers countless entertainment options, from theatres and museums to parks and sports events. Many cultural attractions offer free or discounted entry, and taking advantage of these can help you enjoy the city without breaking the bank.

Salary Expectations

Understanding salary expectations in different industries is key to making informed career decisions in London. The city hosts a diverse range of sectors, each with its own salary norms.

Finance and Banking: London is a global financial hub, and roles in finance and banking are among the highest-paying. Positions in investment banking, asset management, and private equity offer lucrative salaries and bonuses, especially for experienced professionals.

Technology and IT: The tech sector in London is thriving, with many start-ups and established companies offering competitive salaries. Roles in software development, data science, and cybersecurity are particularly well-compensated.

Legal Services: London is home to many prestigious law firms, and legal professionals can command high salaries, particularly in corporate law, intellectual property, and commercial litigation.

Creative Industries: Jobs in the creative sectors, such as media, advertising, and design, offer varied salaries. While entry-level positions may not pay as well, experienced professionals and those in senior roles can earn substantial incomes.

Healthcare and Education: Roles in healthcare and education, including doctors, nurses, and teachers, offer stable but relatively lower salaries compared to sectors like finance or technology. However, these roles often come with strong job security and additional benefits.

Taxation

Navigating the UK's tax system is essential for managing your finances effectively. Here's a brief overview of the key taxes you need to be aware of:

Income Tax: The UK operates a progressive tax system. Your income is taxed at different rates depending on your earnings. For the 2023/2024 tax year, the rates are:

Personal Allowance (up to £12,570): 0%
Basic Rate (£12,571 to £50,270): 20%
Higher Rate (£50,271 to £125,140): 40%
Additional Rate (over £125,140): 45%
National Insurance Contributions (NICs): These are payments made to qualify for certain benefits, including the state pension. The rates vary depending on your employment status and income level.

Council Tax: This is a local tax on residential properties, calculated based on the property's valuation band and the local council's rate.

Value Added Tax (VAT): VAT is added to most goods and services at a standard rate of 20%. Some items are charged at a reduced rate of 5%, or are exempt.

Capital Gains Tax (CGT): This tax is charged on the profit made from selling assets, such as property or shares, above a certain allowance.

Managing Taxes

Understand Your Allowances: Make sure you are aware of all your tax allowances and reliefs, such as the Personal Allowance and the Marriage Allowance. These can significantly reduce your tax bill.

Keep Accurate Records: Maintain detailed records of your income, expenses, and any other financial transactions. This will make it easier to complete your tax return accurately and claim any allowable expenses.

Use Tax-Efficient Investments: Consider using tax-efficient investment vehicles such as ISAs (Individual Savings Accounts) and pensions, which offer tax advantages.

Seek Professional Advice: If your financial situation is complex, consider consulting a tax advisor to help you navigate the tax system and ensure you are paying the right amount.

Conclusion

Navigating London's financial landscape requires a clear understanding of the costs involved, salary expectations, and the tax system. By being well-informed and proactive, you can manage your finances effectively and make the most of the opportunities that London offers.

ENTREPRENEURSHIP IN LONDON

Starting a Business

London is a thriving hub for entrepreneurs, offering a dynamic environment for starting and growing a business. However, the journey from idea to successful enterprise requires careful planning, determination, and a keen understanding of the market.

Identify a Viable Business Idea: The first step is to identify a business idea that meets a market need. Conduct thorough market research to understand your target audience, competitors, and potential demand for your product or service.

Create a Business Plan: A solid business plan is essential for guiding your business and securing funding. Your plan should include:

Executive Summary: A brief overview of your business idea, goals, and strategy.

Market Analysis: Insights into your target market, industry trends, and competitive landscape.

Business Model: Details of how your business will generate revenue and make a profit.

Marketing Strategy: Plans for promoting your business and attracting customers.

Operational Plan: Information on your business operations, including location, suppliers, and staffing.

Financial Plan: Projections for revenue, expenses, and profitability, along with funding requirements.

Register Your Business: Choose a suitable legal structure for your business, such as a sole trader, partnership, or limited company. Register your business with Companies House and obtain any necessary licenses or permits.

Set Up Your Finances: Open a business bank account and set up a robust accounting system to manage your finances. Consider hiring an accountant or using accounting software to keep track of income, expenses, and taxes.

Find the Right Location: Whether you need office space, a retail location, or a workshop, finding the right premises is crucial. Consider factors such as accessibility, cost, and proximity to your target market.

Funding Options

Securing adequate funding is often one of the biggest challenges for new businesses. Fortunately, London offers various funding options to help entrepreneurs get started.

Bootstrapping: Using personal savings and reinvesting profits to fund your business can help you maintain control and avoid debt. However, this approach may limit your initial growth potential.

Bank Loans: Traditional bank loans are a common funding source. To secure a loan, you'll need a strong business plan, good credit history, and potentially some form of collateral.

Venture Capital: Venture capitalists (VCs) provide funding in exchange for equity in your business. This option is suitable for high-growth start-ups with significant potential. VCs often provide valuable industry connections and mentorship.

Angel Investors: Angel investors are individuals who invest their own money in start-ups. They typically offer smaller amounts than VCs but can be more flexible and provide valuable guidance and support.

Crowdfunding: Platforms like Kickstarter and Crowdcube allow you to raise funds from a large number of people. Crowdfunding can also help validate your business idea and build a customer base.

Grants and Government Support: Various grants and government schemes are available to support new businesses. These funds do not need to be repaid and can be a valuable source of capital.

Success Stories

London is home to numerous entrepreneurial success stories that can provide inspiration and insights for your journey.

BrewDog: Founded in 2007, BrewDog started as a small brewery and has grown into a global brand. Their success is attributed to their unique marketing strategies, quality products, and community engagement through equity crowdfunding.

Monzo: Monzo, a digital bank, was launched in 2015 and has rapidly grown to become one of the UK's leading fintech companies. Their focus on user-friendly technology and transparency has attracted a loyal customer base and significant investment.

Deliveroo: Founded in 2013, Deliveroo has revolutionised the food delivery industry. Their innovative logistics model and partnerships with restaurants have driven rapid growth and international expansion.

Gymshark: Started in 2012 by a young entrepreneur, Gymshark has become a leading fitness apparel brand. Their success is driven by effective use of social media marketing and influencer partnerships.

Practical Tips for Entrepreneurs

Start Small and Scale: Begin with a minimum viable product (MVP) to test your idea with real customers. Gather feedback and make improvements before scaling up.

Focus on Customer Experience: Providing excellent customer service can set you apart from competitors and build a loyal customer base.

Leverage Technology: Utilise digital tools and platforms to streamline operations, reach customers, and enhance your business processes.

Network Actively: Building a strong network can provide valuable support, advice, and opportunities for collaboration.

Stay Resilient: Entrepreneurship involves ups and downs. Stay resilient, learn from failures, and keep adapting to changing circumstances.

Conclusion

Starting and growing a business in London is an exciting and challenging endeavour. By identifying a viable business idea, creating a solid plan, securing funding, and learning from successful entrepreneurs, you can navigate the entrepreneurial landscape and build a thriving enterprise.

WHERE TO INVEST IN LONDON PROPERTY

Introduction

Investing in property in up-and-coming areas can yield significant returns as these neighbourhoods undergo development and regeneration. London is constantly evolving, with various districts experiencing growth and transformation. This chapter will explore some of the most promising areas in London where property prices are expected to rise in the coming years.

1. Barking and Dagenham

Barking and Dagenham are undergoing significant regeneration, making them attractive options for property investment.

Regeneration Projects: Major projects like the Barking Riverside development are transforming the area with new homes, schools, healthcare facilities, and transport links.

Transport Improvements: The extension of the Overground line and plans for a new Thames crossing will enhance connectivity, making the area more accessible.

Affordability: Property prices in Barking and Dagenham are relatively affordable compared to central London, offering great potential for growth.

2. Woolwich

Woolwich is another area experiencing rapid development and regeneration.

Crossrail (Elizabeth Line): The opening of the Elizabeth Line has significantly improved transport links, reducing travel times to central London and attracting new residents and businesses.

Riverside Development: The Royal Arsenal Riverside development is transforming Woolwich into a vibrant riverside community with new homes, shops, restaurants, and cultural spaces.

Cultural Hub: Woolwich Works, a new cultural district, aims to enhance the area's cultural and social appeal, attracting more visitors and residents.

3. Nine Elms
Nine Elms is undergoing one of the largest regeneration projects in Europe, making it a hotspot for property investment.

Battersea Power Station: The redevelopment of Battersea Power Station is a key component of the Nine Elms regeneration, featuring new homes, offices, retail spaces, and leisure facilities.

Northern Line Extension: The extension of the Northern Line to include Nine Elms and Battersea has improved transport connections, making the area more attractive to commuters.

Embassy Relocations: The relocation of the US Embassy to Nine Elms has increased the area's profile and attracted further investment.

4. Stratford

Stratford has transformed significantly since the 2012 Olympics and continues to be a desirable area for property investment.

Olympic Legacy: The Queen Elizabeth Olympic Park and surrounding developments have created a vibrant community with excellent amenities, green spaces, and sporting facilities.

Transport Links: Stratford boasts excellent transport links, including the Central and Jubilee lines, DLR, Overground, and National Rail services, making it highly accessible.

Commercial Growth: The area is attracting businesses and institutions, including new office spaces, retail developments, and educational institutions like UCL East.

5. Croydon

Croydon is emerging as a key area for property investment due to its ongoing regeneration and development projects.

Regeneration Projects: Major projects like the £5.25 billion Westfield shopping centre and residential developments are transforming Croydon into a thriving urban centre.

Transport Connectivity: Croydon benefits from excellent transport links, including fast trains to central London, trams, and buses, enhancing its appeal to commuters.

Business Hub: The area is becoming a hub for tech companies and start-ups, boosting the local economy and demand for housing.

6. Tottenham

Tottenham is undergoing significant regeneration, making it an attractive area for property investment.

Tottenham Hale: The redevelopment of Tottenham Hale includes new homes, retail spaces, and improved public spaces, enhancing the area's appeal.

Transport Improvements: Upgrades to Tottenham Hale station and the introduction of the Crossrail 2 project will improve connectivity and attract more residents.

Community Initiatives: Local initiatives to enhance education, healthcare, and community facilities are making Tottenham a more desirable place to live.

7. Acton

Acton is benefiting from significant investment and development, making it a promising area for property investment.

Crossrail (Elizabeth Line): The opening of the Elizabeth Line has improved Acton's connectivity, reducing travel times to central London and other key areas.

Residential Developments: Numerous residential developments, including the Acton Gardens project, are providing new homes and revitalising the area.

Cultural and Community Spaces: Investments in local amenities, cultural spaces, and community facilities are enhancing Acton's appeal to families and young professionals.

Conclusion

Investing in up-and-coming areas in London can offer substantial returns as these neighbourhoods develop and regenerate. Barking and Dagenham, Woolwich, Nine Elms, Stratford, Croydon, Tottenham, and Acton are just a few of the promising areas where property prices are expected to rise in the coming years.

By staying informed about regeneration projects, transport improvements, and local developments, you can make strategic property investment decisions and capitalise on the growth potential of these emerging areas.

INVESTING WISELY

Property Market

Investing in property is a popular and often lucrative way to build wealth in London. The city's property market is dynamic and offers various opportunities for investors, from residential buy-to-let properties to commercial real estate.

Buying vs. Renting: Purchasing property can be a sound investment due to the potential for capital appreciation and rental income. However, it requires significant upfront capital and ongoing maintenance costs. Renting, on the other hand, provides flexibility and lower initial costs but does not build equity.

Best Areas for Investment: London's property market varies significantly by location. Prime central areas like Chelsea, Kensington, and Mayfair are known for their high property values and rental yields. Emerging areas like Stratford, Woolwich, and Peckham offer more affordable options with potential for growth due to ongoing regeneration projects and improved transport links.

Please see the chapter prior for more information on investment areas.

Types of Property Investment:

Buy-to-Let: Purchasing a property to rent out can provide a steady income stream. Consider factors like rental demand, property management costs, and tax implications.

Flipping: Buying properties to renovate and sell at a profit can be profitable but requires knowledge of the market, renovation expertise, and careful budgeting.

Commercial Property: Investing in offices, retail spaces, or industrial properties can offer higher yields but may involve more complex management and longer vacancy periods.

Financing Your Investment: Consider various financing options such as mortgages, buy-to-let loans, or using equity from existing properties. Ensure you have a solid understanding of the terms, interest rates, and repayment schedules.

Legal Considerations: Familiarise yourself with property laws, tenancy regulations, and tax obligations. Consult a solicitor to ensure all legal aspects of your investment are handled correctly.

Stock Market

Investing in the stock market can be a powerful way to grow your wealth over the long term. While it involves risks, a well-diversified portfolio can provide significant returns.

Understanding Stocks and Shares: Stocks represent ownership in a company, and shares are units of stock. Investing in stocks means buying shares of a company with the expectation that their value will increase over time.

Types of Investments:

Individual Stocks: Investing in specific companies allows you to potentially earn high returns, but it also carries higher risk.

Mutual Funds and ETFs: These funds pool money from multiple investors to buy a diversified portfolio of stocks. They offer a balanced risk-return profile and professional management.

Bonds: Bonds are fixed-income securities that provide regular interest payments and return the principal at maturity. They are generally lower risk compared to stocks.

Building a Diversified Portfolio: Diversification reduces risk by spreading investments across different asset classes, sectors, and geographies. A mix of stocks, bonds, and other assets can help balance potential returns and risks.

Long-Term vs. Short-Term Investing: Long-term investing involves holding assets for several years to benefit from compounding returns and market growth. Short-term investing, or trading, focuses on capitalising on short-term market fluctuations and requires more active management.

Research and Analysis: Conduct thorough research before investing. Analyse company financials, market trends, and economic indicators. Tools like financial news, stock analysis websites, and professional advisors can provide valuable insights.

Investment Platforms: Choose a reliable investment platform to buy and sell stocks. Look for features like low fees, user-friendly interfaces, and access to a wide range of investments.

Alternative Investments

In addition to property and stocks, alternative investments can diversify your portfolio and offer unique opportunities for growth.

Cryptocurrencies: Digital currencies like Bitcoin and Ethereum have gained popularity for their potential high returns. However, they are highly volatile and speculative. Invest only what you can afford to lose and stay informed about regulatory changes.

Peer-to-Peer Lending: P2P lending platforms allow you to lend money to individuals or small businesses in exchange for interest payments. While they offer attractive returns, they also carry higher risk compared to traditional savings accounts.

Art and Collectibles: Investing in art, antiques, or collectibles can provide substantial returns if you have expertise and a keen eye for valuable items. However, the market can be illiquid, and prices can fluctuate widely.

Venture Capital and Private Equity: Investing in start-ups or private companies can yield high returns if the business succeeds. However, these investments are typically illiquid and high-risk, requiring substantial capital and due diligence.

Real Estate Investment Trusts (REITs): REITs allow you to invest in real estate without directly owning property. They provide regular income through dividends and offer exposure to the property market with greater liquidity.

Risk Management

Investing involves risk, but you can manage and mitigate these risks through careful planning and strategy.

Diversification: Spread your investments across different asset classes, sectors, and geographies to reduce risk.

Regular Reviews: Monitor your investments regularly and adjust your portfolio based on performance and changing market conditions.

Stay Informed: Keep up-to-date with market news, economic indicators, and changes in regulations that may affect your investments.

Professional Advice: Consider consulting financial advisors or investment professionals for tailored advice and strategies.

Conclusion

Investing wisely is a crucial component of wealth building. By understanding the property market, stock market, and alternative investments, you can create a diversified portfolio that balances risk and reward.

EMPLOYMENT STRATEGIES

High-Paying Jobs

Securing a high-paying job in London is a significant step towards building wealth. The city's diverse economy offers numerous opportunities across various industries. Here are some of the top sectors and roles that command attractive salaries:

Finance and Banking: Roles in investment banking, asset management, and corporate finance are highly lucrative. Positions such as investment bankers, financial analysts, and portfolio managers often come with substantial bonuses in addition to their base salaries.

Technology and IT: The tech industry is booming in London. High-demand roles include software developers, data scientists, and cybersecurity experts. Tech companies, ranging from start-ups to global giants, offer competitive salaries and benefits to attract top talent.

Legal Services: Lawyers, especially those specialising in corporate law, intellectual property, and commercial litigation, are well-compensated. Working for top law firms or in-house at major corporations can lead to impressive earnings.

Consulting: Management consultants, particularly those working with leading consulting firms, earn significant salaries. Consultants specialising in strategy, operations, and technology are in high demand.

Medicine and Healthcare: While entry-level positions in healthcare may not be as high-paying, experienced professionals such as surgeons, specialists, and senior consultants can earn substantial incomes. Private healthcare roles often offer higher salaries than NHS positions.

Media and Creative Industries: Senior roles in media, advertising, and design can be highly lucrative. Creative directors, media executives, and experienced professionals in these fields often command impressive salaries.

Networking

Networking is a critical component of career success in London. Building a robust professional network can open doors to job opportunities, mentorship, and industry insights. Here are some effective networking strategies:

Attend Industry Events: Participate in conferences, seminars, and workshops relevant to your field. These events are excellent opportunities to meet industry leaders, potential employers, and like-minded professionals.

Join Professional Associations: Becoming a member of industry-specific associations or groups can provide access to valuable resources, networking events, and professional development opportunities.

Utilise Online Platforms: Leverage platforms like LinkedIn to connect with professionals in your industry. Engage in discussions, share relevant content, and join groups to expand your network.

Seek Mentorship: Identify potential mentors within your industry who can provide guidance, advice, and support. A mentor can offer valuable insights into navigating your career path and achieving your goals.

Volunteer and Give Back: Volunteering for industry events, charities, or professional organisations can help you meet influential people and build a positive reputation within your field.

Job-Hopping vs. Loyalty

Deciding between job-hopping and staying loyal to one employer is a critical consideration for your career strategy in London. Each approach has its pros and cons:

Job-Hopping: Frequently changing jobs can lead to higher salary increments, broader experience, and faster career progression. In dynamic industries like technology and finance, job-hopping is often seen as a way to quickly climb the career ladder. However, it's essential to balance this with the risk of being perceived as unreliable or lacking commitment.

Loyalty: Staying with one employer for an extended period can lead to job security, deeper expertise, and stronger relationships within the company. Long-term loyalty can also result in promotions and internal opportunities. However, it may limit your exposure to new experiences and potentially slow down your salary growth.

Making the Right Choice

Evaluate Your Career Goals: Consider your long-term career objectives. If gaining diverse experiences and rapidly increasing your salary are priorities, job-hopping may be beneficial. If you value stability, deep expertise, and strong relationships, staying loyal might be the better option.

Assess the Company Culture: Some companies reward loyalty with clear career progression and attractive benefits, while others may favour fresh talent and external hires. Understanding the culture of your current or prospective employer can inform your decision.

Seek Advice: Talk to mentors, industry peers, and career advisors to gain insights into the best approach for your specific situation.

Practical Steps to Secure High-Paying Jobs

Enhance Your Skills: Continuously improve your skills through courses, certifications, and professional development. Staying updated with industry trends and acquiring in-demand skills can make you a more attractive candidate.

Tailor Your CV: Customise your CV for each job application to highlight relevant experience and achievements. Use specific examples and metrics to demonstrate your impact.

Prepare for Interviews: Research the company and the role thoroughly. Practise common interview questions and prepare to discuss how your skills and experience align with the job requirements.

Negotiate Your Salary: Don't be afraid to negotiate your salary and benefits. Research industry standards and be prepared to discuss your value and contributions to justify your request.

Leverage Recruiters: Professional recruiters and headhunters can help you find high-paying opportunities and provide valuable insights into the job market.

Conclusion

Navigating the job market in London requires a strategic approach. By targeting high-paying roles, actively networking, and making informed decisions about job-hopping versus loyalty, you can build a successful and lucrative career.

The next chapter will explore entrepreneurship in London, offering insights into starting and growing a business in this dynamic city.

SIDE HUSTLES

The Gig Economy

The gig economy has transformed the way people work, offering flexibility and opportunities to earn extra income. In London, the gig economy is thriving, with numerous platforms and services available for those looking to take on side hustles.

Understanding the Gig Economy: The gig economy involves short-term, flexible jobs or freelance work instead of traditional full-time employment. It includes roles such as delivery drivers, rideshare drivers, freelance writers, and more.

Popular Platforms:

Uber and Bolt: Drive for rideshare companies.

Deliveroo and Uber Eats: Deliver food to customers.

TaskRabbit: Complete various tasks and errands for people.

Fiverr and Upwork: Offer freelance services such as writing, graphic design, and web development.

Benefits:

Flexibility: Set your own hours and choose the projects you work on.

Extra Income: Supplement your primary income with additional earnings.

Skill Development: Gain experience and develop new skills in different areas.

Challenges:

Income Variability: Earnings can fluctuate based on demand and availability.

Lack of Benefits: Gig economy jobs typically do not offer benefits such as health insurance or retirement plans.

Time Management: Balancing multiple gigs with your main job and personal life can be challenging.

Freelancing

Freelancing offers the opportunity to work independently and provide services to multiple clients. It's a popular choice for those with specialised skills who want to control their work environment and schedule.

Identifying Your Skills: Determine the skills you can offer as a freelancer, such as writing, graphic design, programming, consulting, or marketing.

Building a Portfolio: Create a portfolio showcasing your best work to attract potential clients. Include examples of completed projects, client testimonials, and any relevant qualifications or certifications.

Finding Clients: Use platforms like LinkedIn, Upwork, Fiverr, and Freelancer to find clients. Networking, attending industry events, and leveraging social media can also help you secure projects.

Setting Rates: Research industry standards to set competitive rates. Consider your experience, the complexity of the work, and the value you provide to clients.

Managing Your Business:

Contracts: Always use contracts to outline the scope of work, payment terms, and deadlines.

Invoicing: Use invoicing software to manage payments and track income.

Time Management: Organise your schedule to meet deadlines and maintain a healthy work-life balance.

Scaling Your Freelance Business: As you gain more clients and experience, consider expanding your services, increasing your rates, or hiring additional freelancers to help with larger projects.

Passive Income Streams

Creating passive income streams is a powerful way to generate money with minimal ongoing effort. While some passive income ideas require initial investment and time, they can provide long-term financial benefits.

Rental Properties: Investing in rental properties can provide a steady income stream. Ensure you understand the responsibilities of being a landlord, including property maintenance and tenant management.

Dividend Stocks: Invest in dividend-paying stocks to receive regular income from your investments. Research companies with a strong track record of dividend payments.

Peer-to-Peer Lending: Platforms like Funding Circle and RateSetter allow you to lend money to individuals or small businesses in exchange for interest payments.

Royalties: Create intellectual property such as books, music, or online courses that generate royalties. Platforms like Amazon Kindle Direct Publishing,

Udemy, and Teachable can help you reach a wide audience.

Affiliate Marketing: Promote products or services through affiliate marketing programs and earn commissions on sales. Build a website, blog, or social media presence to attract an audience.

Investing in Index Funds: Index funds track a specific market index and provide broad market exposure with minimal management. They offer a relatively low-risk way to invest and generate returns over time.

Practical Tips for Success

Set Clear Goals: Define your objectives for your side hustles and passive income streams. Whether it's paying off debt, saving for a major purchase, or achieving financial independence, having clear goals will keep you motivated.

Balance Your Time: Managing a side hustle alongside a full-time job requires effective time management. Use tools like calendars, to-do lists, and time-tracking apps to stay organised.

Stay Consistent: Consistency is key to success in any endeavour. Dedicate regular time to your side hustle or passive income projects to ensure steady progress.

Educate Yourself: Continuously learn and improve your skills. Take advantage of online courses, books, and workshops to enhance your knowledge and stay competitive.

Network with Others: Connect with other gig workers, freelancers, and investors. Join online forums, attend meetups, and participate in professional groups to share experiences and gain insights.

Monitor Your Finances: Keep track of your income and expenses from your side hustles and investments. Use financial software or hire an accountant to manage your finances effectively.

Conclusion

Side hustles and passive income streams offer excellent opportunities to boost your earnings and achieve financial goals. By leveraging the gig economy, freelancing, and investing in passive income sources, you can create multiple streams of income and enhance your financial security.

50 WAYS TO MAKE MONEY ONLINE

The digital age has opened up countless opportunities for making money online. Whether you're looking for a side hustle, a part-time job, or a full-fledged business, there's something for everyone. This chapter explores 50 ways to make money online in 2024 and 2025, catering to various skills, interests, and levels of commitment.

Freelancing

Freelance Writing: Offer your writing services for blogs, websites, and publications. Platforms like Upwork, Fiverr, and Freelancer are great places to start.

Graphic Design: Create logos, social media graphics, and marketing materials for clients. Use platforms like 99designs and DesignCrowd.

Web Development: Build websites and web applications for businesses and individuals. Specialise in popular platforms like WordPress or coding languages like HTML, CSS, and JavaScript.

Video Editing: Edit videos for YouTube creators, businesses, and marketers. Use software like Adobe Premiere Pro or Final Cut Pro.

Social Media Management: Manage social media accounts for businesses and influencers. Create content, schedule posts, and engage with followers.

Virtual Assistance: Provide administrative support to businesses remotely. Tasks can include email management, scheduling, and data entry.

SEO Consulting: Help websites improve their search engine rankings through SEO strategies and techniques.

Copywriting: Write persuasive sales copy for websites, ads, and email marketing campaigns.

Translation Services: Translate documents and content between different languages. Platforms like ProZ and TranslatorsCafe can help you find clients.

Voiceover Work: Provide voiceover services for commercials, audiobooks, and videos.

Online Teaching and Tutoring

Online Tutoring: Teach subjects like math, science, or languages to students worldwide. Websites like Tutor.com and Chegg Tutors can connect you with students.

Teaching English Online: Teach English to non-native speakers through platforms like VIPKid, iTalki, and Cambly.

Course Creation: Create and sell online courses on platforms like Udemy, Teachable, and Coursera.

Music Lessons: Teach music theory, instruments, or vocal lessons online.

Fitness Coaching: Offer personalised fitness training and nutrition advice through video calls and online programs.

E-commerce

Dropshipping: Start an online store without holding inventory. Use platforms like Shopify and Oberlo to manage your dropshipping business.

Print on Demand: Create custom designs for products like t-shirts, mugs, and phone cases. Sell them through platforms like Printful and Redbubble.

Etsy Shop: Sell handmade crafts, vintage items, or digital downloads on Etsy.

Amazon FBA: Use Amazon's Fulfilled by Amazon (FBA) program to sell products without handling shipping and customer service.

E-commerce Store: Launch your own online store using platforms like Shopify, WooCommerce, or BigCommerce.

Digital Products

E-books: Write and sell e-books on platforms like Amazon Kindle Direct Publishing (KDP) and Smashwords.

Stock Photography: Sell your photos on stock photography websites like Shutterstock, Adobe Stock, and iStock.

Graphic Templates: Create and sell templates for websites, social media, and marketing materials on platforms like Creative Market and Envato.

Music Production: Create and sell music tracks, beats, and sound effects on websites like AudioJungle and BeatStars.

App Development: Develop and sell mobile apps or games on the Apple App Store and Google Play Store.

Blogging and Content Creation

Blogging: Start a blog on a topic you're passionate about. Monetise through ads, sponsored posts, and affiliate marketing.

YouTube Channel: Create a YouTube channel and earn money through ads, sponsorships, and merchandise sales.

Podcasting: Start a podcast and monetise through sponsorships, donations, and merchandise.

Affiliate Marketing: Promote products and earn a commission for each sale made through your referral links. Join affiliate programs on platforms like Amazon Associates and ShareASale.

Influencer Marketing: Build a social media following and collaborate with brands for sponsored posts and product promotions.

Investing

Stock Trading: Buy and sell stocks through online brokerage accounts. Educate yourself on market trends and strategies.

Cryptocurrency Trading: Trade cryptocurrencies like Bitcoin and Ethereum on platforms like Binance and Coinbase.

Real Estate Crowdfunding: Invest in real estate projects through crowdfunding platforms like Fundrise and RealtyMogul.

Peer-to-Peer Lending: Lend money to individuals or small businesses through platforms like LendingClub and Prosper, and earn interest on your loans.

Robo-Advisors: Use robo-advisors like Betterment and Wealthfront to manage and grow your investment portfolio automatically.

Miscellaneous

Online Surveys: Earn money by taking surveys on websites like Swagbucks, Survey Junkie, and Vindale Research.

User Testing: Test websites and apps for usability and provide feedback. Platforms like UserTesting and TryMyUI pay for your insights.

Freelance Writing: Write articles, blog posts, and other content for websites and publications. Platforms like Medium Partner Program pay writers based on reader engagement.

Domain Flipping: Buy and sell domain names for a profit. Use marketplaces like Flippa to find and trade domains.

Remote Customer Service: Work as a remote customer service representative for companies. Platforms like Remote.co and FlexJobs list such opportunities.

Website Flipping: Buy, improve, and sell websites for a profit. Platforms like Flippa and Empire Flippers facilitate website trading.

Dropshipping: Start an e-commerce business where you sell products without holding inventory. Use platforms like Shopify and Oberlo.

Social Media Management: Manage social media accounts for businesses and individuals, creating content and engaging with followers.

Online Workshops and Webinars: Host paid online workshops or webinars on topics you're knowledgeable about.

Freelance Coding: Offer coding services for websites, apps, and software projects. Platforms like Toptal and Stack Overflow Jobs can connect you with clients.

Virtual Event Planning: Plan and coordinate virtual events such as conferences, webinars, and online meetups.

Online Market Trading: Trade commodities, forex, or other financial instruments on platforms like E*TRADE and TD Ameritrade.

Freelance Illustration: Create custom illustrations and artwork for clients. Platforms like ArtStation and DeviantArt offer marketplaces for artists.

Online Consulting: Provide expert advice in your field of expertise, such as business, marketing, or technology.

Online Marketplaces: Sell products on online marketplaces like eBay, Gumtree, and Facebook Marketplace.

Conclusion

The internet provides countless opportunities to make money online in 2024. Whether you prefer freelancing, teaching, e-commerce, investing, or content creation, there's a method that suits your skills and interests.

By exploring these 50 ways to earn money online, you can find the right fit for your lifestyle and financial goals. Embrace the digital age, leverage your talents, and start building your online income streams today.

FINANCIAL MANAGEMENT

Budgeting Tips

Effective financial management begins with a well-structured budget. Budgeting helps you track your income and expenses, ensuring you live within your means and make informed financial decisions.

Track Your Income and Expenses: Start by documenting all sources of income, including your salary, freelance earnings, and any passive income. Next, track your expenses, categorising them into essential (rent, utilities, groceries) and non-essential (entertainment, dining out).

Set Financial Goals: Define short-term and long-term financial goals. Short-term goals might include saving for a holiday or paying off a credit card, while long-term goals could involve buying a home or building a retirement fund.

Create a Budget Plan: Allocate your income to cover essential expenses first, then distribute the remaining funds towards your financial goals and non-essential spending. Tools like budgeting apps (e.g., YNAB, Mint) or simple spreadsheets can help you create and stick to your budget.

Use the 50/30/20 Rule: This budgeting method allocates 50% of your income to necessities, 30% to discretionary spending, and 20% to savings and debt repayment. Adjust the percentages based on your personal financial situation.

Regularly Review Your Budget: Revisit your budget monthly to ensure you stay on track. Adjust your plan as necessary to accommodate changes in income or unexpected expenses.

Saving Strategies

Saving money is crucial for financial stability and achieving your goals. Implementing effective saving strategies can help you build an emergency fund, save for significant expenses, and secure your future.

Automate Savings: Set up automatic transfers from your current account to your savings account. Automating savings ensures you consistently save a portion of your income without having to think about it.

Create an Emergency Fund: Aim to save three to six months' worth of living expenses in an easily accessible account. An emergency fund provides a financial cushion in case of unexpected expenses or job loss.

Take Advantage of High-Interest Accounts: Utilise savings accounts with higher interest rates to maximise your returns. Consider options like ISAs (Individual Savings Accounts) that offer tax-free interest.

Cut Unnecessary Expenses: Review your spending habits and identify areas where you can cut back. Simple changes, like making coffee at home instead of buying it daily or cancelling unused subscriptions, can add up over time.

Set Savings Goals: Define specific savings goals for short-term and long-term objectives. Having clear goals, such as saving for a new car or a home deposit, can motivate you to stay disciplined.

Debt Management

Managing debt effectively is essential to maintaining financial health. By adopting smart strategies, you can reduce your debt burden and improve your financial situation.

List All Debts: Make a comprehensive list of all your debts, including credit cards, loans, and mortgages. Note the interest rates, minimum payments, and outstanding balances for each.

Prioritise High-Interest Debt: Focus on paying off high-interest debt first, such as credit card balances. This approach reduces the overall interest you pay and helps you become debt-free faster.

Consider Debt Consolidation: If you have multiple debts, consolidating them into a single loan with a lower interest rate can simplify your payments and potentially reduce the interest you pay.

Use the Snowball Method: The snowball method involves paying off the smallest debt first while making minimum payments on larger debts. Once the smallest debt is paid off, move on to the next smallest. This method can build momentum and motivation as you eliminate debts one by one.

Negotiate with Creditors: If you're struggling to make payments, contact your creditors to discuss your options. They may offer reduced interest rates, extended payment terms, or other arrangements to help you manage your debt.

Avoid Taking on New Debt: Focus on paying down existing debt before taking on new loans or credit cards. Avoid using credit for non-essential purchases.

Practical Tips for Financial Management

Use Financial Tools: Leverage budgeting apps, online calculators, and financial planning software to manage your money effectively. These tools can provide insights, track progress, and help you make informed decisions.

Educate Yourself: Continuously learn about personal finance through books, online courses, and financial news. Understanding financial concepts and staying informed can help you make better financial decisions.

Seek Professional Advice: Consider consulting a financial advisor for personalised guidance. An advisor can help you create a comprehensive financial plan, manage investments, and navigate complex financial situations.

Maintain a Healthy Credit Score: Your credit score affects your ability to borrow money and the interest rates you receive. Pay bills on time, keep credit card balances low, and avoid applying for too much credit to maintain a good score.

Plan for Retirement: Start saving for retirement as early as possible. Contribute to pension schemes or personal retirement accounts, and take advantage of employer-matched contributions if available.

Review Your Financial Plan Regularly: Life circumstances and financial goals can change over time. Regularly review and adjust your financial plan to ensure it remains aligned with your objectives.

Conclusion

Effective financial management is the cornerstone of building and maintaining wealth. By mastering budgeting, saving, and debt management, you can achieve financial stability and work towards your goals.

The next chapter will explore leveraging technology to enhance your financial management, providing insights into financial apps, online learning, and automation tools that can streamline your journey to wealth.

LEVERAGING TECHNOLOGY

Financial Apps

In the digital age, technology plays a crucial role in managing personal finances. A variety of financial apps are available to help you track spending, manage investments, and save money efficiently.

Budgeting Apps:

YNAB (You Need A Budget): This app helps you create a detailed budget, track your expenses, and set financial goals. Its proactive approach encourages you to plan your spending and save more effectively.

Mint: Mint aggregates all your financial accounts in one place, allowing you to track income, expenses, and budgeting goals. It offers personalised tips and alerts to help you stay on track.

Savings Apps:

Monzo: Monzo is a digital bank that offers budgeting tools, saving pots, and spending analytics. Its easy-to-use interface and real-time notifications make managing money simple and effective.

Starling Bank: Another popular digital bank, Starling offers fee-free spending abroad, savings goals, and insightful spending summaries to help you manage your finances.

Investment Apps:

Nutmeg: Nutmeg provides online investment management services, including ISAs and pensions. It offers personalised portfolios based on your risk tolerance and investment goals.

Freetrade: Freetrade is a commission-free trading app that allows you to invest in stocks, ETFs, and investment trusts. Its user-friendly design makes it easy for beginners to start investing.

Debt Management Apps:

Debt Payoff Planner: This app helps you create a plan to pay off your debts efficiently. It allows you to track your progress and offers various payoff strategies, including the snowball and avalanche methods.

Tally: Tally is a debt management app that helps you pay off credit card debt faster by optimising payments and reducing interest.

Expense Tracking Apps:

Expensify: Ideal for both personal and business use, Expensify tracks receipts, mileage, and expenses. It simplifies the process of expense reporting and reimbursement.

Splitwise: Splitwise is great for managing shared expenses, whether you're splitting bills with roommates or sharing costs with friends. It keeps track of who owes what and makes settling up easy.

Online Learning

Continual learning is essential for staying ahead in today's fast-paced financial world. Online learning platforms offer a wealth of resources to help you enhance your financial literacy and skills.

Coursera: Coursera offers a wide range of finance and investment courses from top universities and institutions. Courses like "Financial Markets" by Yale University or "Introduction to Corporate Finance" by the University of Pennsylvania provide valuable insights.

Udemy: Udemy provides courses on various aspects of personal finance, investing, and business management. Look for highly rated courses like "Personal Finance 101: Everything You Need to Know" or "Stock Market Investing for Beginners."

edX: Similar to Coursera, edX offers courses from renowned institutions. Courses such as "Fundamentals of Personal Finance" by Purdue University or "Investment Strategies and Portfolio Analysis" by the New York Institute of Finance can help deepen your knowledge.

Khan Academy: Khan Academy offers free courses on personal finance, economics, and investing. Its easy-to-understand format makes it accessible for learners at all levels.

LinkedIn Learning: LinkedIn Learning provides courses on financial planning, investing, and career development. Courses like "Financial Literacy: How to Gain Financial Knowledge and Use it in Your Life" can be particularly beneficial.

Automation

Automating your finances can save time, reduce errors, and ensure you stay on track with your financial goals. Here are some ways to leverage automation effectively:

Automated Savings: Set up automatic transfers from your current account to your savings account. Many banks and apps, like Monzo and Starling, offer features to automate regular savings.

Bill Payments: Automate recurring bill payments to avoid late fees and ensure timely payments. Most utility providers and service companies offer options for automatic payments.

Investment Contributions: Automate contributions to your investment accounts, such as pensions or ISAs. Regular, automatic contributions can help you take advantage of pound-cost averaging and build wealth steadily over time.

Expense Tracking: Use apps like Mint or YNAB to automatically categorise and track your expenses. This helps you stay within your budget and identify areas where you can cut back.

Debt Repayment: Automate your debt repayments to ensure you never miss a payment. Many debt management apps and financial institutions offer options to set up automatic payments.

Financial Alerts: Set up alerts for account balances, due dates, and unusual activity. Apps and online banking services can send notifications to keep you informed and help prevent fraud.

Practical Tips for Leveraging Technology

Choose the Right Tools: Select financial apps and tools that best meet your needs and preferences. Read reviews, compare features, and try out free versions before committing to a particular app.

Stay Secure: Ensure that the apps and platforms you use have strong security measures in place. Use complex passwords, enable two-factor authentication, and regularly monitor your accounts for any suspicious activity.

Keep Learning: Stay updated on the latest financial tools and technologies. Regularly explore new apps, features, and educational resources to enhance your financial management.

Integrate Your Systems: Where possible, integrate your financial apps and accounts for a seamless experience. For example, link your budgeting app to your bank account for real-time updates.

Review and Adjust: Periodically review your automated systems and financial tools to ensure they are still meeting your needs. Adjust settings and strategies as your financial situation and goals evolve.

Conclusion

Leveraging technology can significantly enhance your financial management by providing convenient, efficient, and effective tools. From budgeting apps and online learning platforms to automated savings and investment contributions, technology offers numerous ways to streamline your financial journey.

SAVE SOME CASH

Introduction

Living in London can be expensive, but with some strategic planning and smart choices, you can significantly reduce your commuting and day-to-day costs. Even though this book is about getting rich, by cutting costs on the basic things, you have more money to invest in real opportunities that stand to make you real money.

This chapter provides practical tips and advice on how to save money while navigating the city's expenses.

Saving on Commuting Costs

Use an Oyster Card or Contactless Payment: Oyster cards and contactless payment methods offer discounted fares compared to buying single tickets. They also cap daily and weekly travel costs, helping you save money.

Travel at Off-Peak Times: Off-peak fares are cheaper than peak-time fares. If your schedule allows, try to travel during off-peak hours to save on your commute.

Buy a Travelcard: If you travel frequently, consider purchasing a Travelcard. It offers unlimited travel within certain zones and can be more cost-effective than paying for individual journeys.

Cycle to Work: Cycling is a great way to save on commuting costs while getting some exercise. London has an extensive network of cycle routes and bike-sharing schemes like Santander Cycles.

Walk When Possible: Walking is free and can often be quicker than taking public transport for short journeys. Use apps like Citymapper to find the best walking routes.

Use Railcards: Railcards like the 16-25 Railcard, 26-30 Railcard, and Network Railcard offer significant discounts on train fares. Check if you're eligible and take advantage of the savings.

Carpool: If you need to drive, consider carpooling with colleagues or friends. You can share fuel and parking costs, making it a more economical option.

Telecommute: If your job allows, working from home even a few days a week can save you a significant amount on commuting costs.

Saving on Day-to-Day Costs

Meal Prep: Preparing your meals at home is much cheaper than eating out. Plan your meals for the week, cook in bulk, and take packed lunches to work.

Use Discount Supermarkets: Shop at discount supermarkets like Aldi and Lidl, which often offer lower prices than major chains. Buying in bulk and looking for special offers can also help reduce your grocery bill.

Take Advantage of Loyalty Schemes: Many supermarkets and retailers offer loyalty schemes that provide discounts, cashback, and special offers. Sign up for these programs to save on your purchases.

Buy Own-Brand Products: Own-brand products are usually cheaper than branded items and often just as good in quality. Opt for these products to save money on groceries and household essentials.

Use Coupons and Vouchers: Look for coupons and vouchers in newspapers, magazines, and online. Websites like VoucherCodes and Groupon offer discounts on a wide range of products and services.

Limit Takeaway Coffee: Instead of buying coffee on the go, make your own at home or work. If you do buy coffee, consider bringing your own reusable cup, as many cafes offer discounts for this.

Utilise Free Activities: London has plenty of free activities and attractions, such as museums, galleries, parks, and walking tours. Take advantage of these free options for entertainment and leisure.

Shop Second-Hand: Second-hand shops, charity shops, and online marketplaces like eBay and Gumtree offer great deals on clothing, furniture, and electronics.

Monitor Utility Bills: Regularly review your utility bills and switch providers if you find a better deal. Websites like Uswitch can help you compare and switch to cheaper energy, broadband, and insurance providers.

Reduce Energy Usage: Save on energy bills by turning off lights and appliances when not in use, using energy-efficient bulbs, and insulating your home properly.

Maximising Discounts and Offers

Student Discounts: If you're a student, make the most of student discounts available at many retailers, restaurants, and service providers. Websites like UNiDAYS and Student Beans list numerous discounts.

Workplace Benefits: Check if your employer offers benefits such as discounted gym memberships, cycle-to-work schemes, or travel loans.

Local Deals: Keep an eye out for local deals and offers. Sign up for newsletters from your favourite stores and restaurants to receive exclusive discounts and promotions.

London Pass: If you enjoy visiting attractions, consider purchasing a London Pass. It offers free entry to many top attractions and can save you money if you plan to visit several places.

Membership Discounts: Join membership clubs or organisations that offer discounts on a range of services and products, such as the National Trust or English Heritage.

Practical Tips for Saving Money

Create a Budget: Track your income and expenses to identify areas where you can cut costs. Use budgeting apps like YNAB or Mint to help you manage your finances.

Plan Your Shopping: Make a shopping list before you go to the store and stick to it. Avoid impulse purchases and take advantage of sales and promotions on items you regularly use.

Cook at Home: Eating out can be expensive, so try to cook at home as much as possible. Experiment with new recipes and make cooking a fun and enjoyable activity.

Use Public Libraries: Public libraries offer free access to books, magazines, and online resources. They also often host free events and workshops.

Track Subscriptions: Review your subscriptions and cancel any that you don't use regularly. This includes streaming services, gym memberships, and magazine subscriptions.

Shop Seasonally: Buy fruits and vegetables that are in season, as they are often cheaper and fresher. Visit local markets for good deals on fresh produce.

DIY Repairs: Learn basic DIY skills to handle minor home repairs yourself instead of hiring professionals. YouTube tutorials and online guides can be very helpful.

Conclusion

Living in London doesn't have to be prohibitively expensive. By making smart choices and taking advantage of discounts, offers, and cost-saving strategies, you can significantly reduce your commuting and day-to-day expenses. Implementing these tips will help you enjoy all that London has to offer while keeping your finances in check.

NETWORKING AND MENTORSHIP

Finding Mentors

A mentor can provide invaluable guidance, support, and insights based on their own experiences. Building a relationship with a mentor can accelerate your financial and career growth.

Identify Your Needs: Determine what you hope to gain from a mentorship relationship. Are you looking for career advice, financial guidance, or personal development? Knowing your needs will help you find the right mentor.

Look Within Your Network: Start by looking within your existing network. Reach out to colleagues, managers, or industry professionals you admire. Attending industry events and conferences can also help you connect with potential mentors.

Use Professional Associations: Many professional organisations offer mentorship programs. Joining associations related to your field can provide access to experienced professionals who are willing to mentor.

Online Platforms: Platforms like LinkedIn can be useful for finding mentors. Engage with thought leaders and professionals in your field by commenting on their posts and sending personalised connection requests.

Be Clear and Respectful: When approaching potential mentors, be clear about what you are looking for and respectful of their time. Explain why you admire them and how their guidance could benefit you.

Formalise the Relationship: Once you have identified a mentor, set clear expectations and goals for the mentorship. Regularly scheduled meetings and defined objectives can help make the relationship productive and mutually beneficial.

Professional Organisations

Joining professional organisations can enhance your network, provide learning opportunities, and increase your visibility in your industry.

Industry Associations: Many industries have professional associations that offer networking events, conferences, and training. Examples include the Chartered Institute of Personnel and Development (CIPD) for HR professionals or the Institute of Chartered Accountants in England and Wales (ICAEW) for accountants.

Networking Events: Attend networking events hosted by these organisations. These events provide opportunities to meet industry leaders, share knowledge, and explore potential collaborations.

Workshops and Seminars: Participate in workshops and seminars to develop your skills and stay updated on industry trends. These events also offer networking opportunities.

Volunteer Opportunities: Volunteering for roles within professional organisations can increase your visibility and allow you to develop leadership skills while expanding your network.

Online Communities: Many professional organisations have online forums or social media groups where members can share information, seek advice, and network virtually.

Building Relationships

Building strong professional relationships is essential for long-term success. These relationships can provide support, open doors to new opportunities, and offer diverse perspectives.

Be Genuine: Authenticity is key to building strong relationships. Show genuine interest in others and be yourself in your interactions.

Offer Value: Networking should be a two-way street. Offer help, share knowledge, and provide value to your connections. Building a reputation as a helpful and resourceful person can lead to stronger relationships.

Follow Up: After meeting someone new, follow up with a thank-you message or connect on LinkedIn. Keeping in touch helps maintain the relationship and shows that you value the connection.

Stay in Touch: Regularly check in with your network, even when you don't need anything. Sharing updates, congratulating people on their achievements, and offering help can keep your relationships strong.

Be a Good Listener: Show interest in others by actively listening to them. Understanding their needs, challenges, and goals can help you find ways to support them and strengthen your connection.

Attend Social Events: Social events, both professional and informal, offer opportunities to build relationships. Engage in conversations, share experiences, and connect with people on a personal level.

Leveraging Your Network

Once you have built a strong network, it's important to leverage it effectively to achieve your goals.

Seek Advice: Don't hesitate to ask for advice or insights from your network. Experienced professionals can provide valuable perspectives on career decisions, financial strategies, and personal growth.

Explore Collaborations: Look for opportunities to collaborate with people in your network. Joint ventures, partnerships, and project collaborations can lead to new opportunities and mutual benefits.

Find Job Opportunities: Many job opportunities come through referrals and recommendations. Let your network know when you are looking for new opportunities, and be open to referrals.

Gain Exposure: Leverage your network to increase your visibility. Speaking at events, contributing to industry publications, and participating in webinars can help establish you as a thought leader.

Support Others: Be proactive in supporting your network. Recommending people for opportunities, endorsing their skills on LinkedIn, and providing testimonials can strengthen your relationships and create a supportive community.

Practical Tips for Effective Networking

Set Networking Goals: Define what you want to achieve through networking. Whether it's finding a mentor, exploring career opportunities, or gaining industry insights, having clear goals can guide your efforts.

Prepare Your Elevator Pitch: Have a concise and engaging introduction ready that explains who you are, what you do, and what you're looking for. This can make networking conversations more effective.

Use Social Media Wisely: Social media platforms like LinkedIn and Twitter are powerful tools for networking. Share relevant content, engage with others' posts, and participate in discussions to build your online presence.

Be Consistent: Networking is not a one-time activity. Consistently engage with your network, attend events, and seek new connections to keep your network dynamic and growing.

Stay Organised: Keep track of your contacts, interactions, and follow-ups. Using a CRM tool or a simple spreadsheet can help you manage your network effectively.

Be Patient: Building a strong network takes time. Be patient and persistent, and focus on building genuine, long-lasting relationships rather than seeking immediate benefits.

Conclusion

Networking and mentorship are powerful tools for achieving financial and career success. By finding the right mentors, joining professional organisations, building strong relationships, and leveraging your network, you can unlock new opportunities and gain valuable support.

The next chapter will focus on maintaining a balanced life, exploring strategies to ensure health, happiness, and fulfilment while pursuing wealth.

LIVING LIKE A MILLIONAIRE IN LONDON

Introduction

London, with its rich history, cultural vibrancy, and cosmopolitan lifestyle, offers countless opportunities to live a luxurious and fulfilling life. Whether you're already a millionaire or aspire to live like one, this chapter will guide you through the best ways to enjoy the opulent lifestyle that London has to offer.

Prime Residential Areas

Living in one of London's most prestigious neighbourhoods is a key part of the millionaire lifestyle. These areas offer not only luxurious properties but also a high quality of life, with access to top-notch amenities and services.

Kensington and Chelsea: Known for their grand Victorian townhouses, garden squares, and proximity to Hyde Park, these neighbourhoods are among the most desirable in London. Exclusive shops, Michelin-starred restaurants, and cultural institutions like the Victoria and Albert Museum add to the allure.

Mayfair: With its elegant Georgian architecture, high-end boutiques, and proximity to Buckingham Palace, Mayfair epitomises luxury. It's home to some of London's most prestigious hotels, private members' clubs, and fine dining establishments.

Belgravia: This affluent area is characterised by its white stucco terraces and garden squares. It offers a tranquil, village-like atmosphere while being just a stone's throw from the bustling city centre.

Hampstead: Known for its leafy streets, period homes, and expansive Heath, Hampstead offers a blend of rural charm and urban sophistication. It's a popular choice for affluent families and celebrities.

Exclusive Dining Experiences

London boasts an impressive array of world-class restaurants, offering everything from traditional British fare to international cuisine. For a true millionaire experience, consider dining at these top establishments.

The Ledbury: Located in Notting Hill, The Ledbury offers exquisite modern European cuisine in an elegant setting. Its two Michelin stars are a testament to its exceptional quality and service.

Dinner by Heston Blumenthal: Situated in Knightsbridge, this restaurant offers a unique dining experience inspired by historic British gastronomy. The innovative menu and stylish ambiance make it a favourite among the elite.

Sketch: This Mayfair hotspot combines art, music, and gastronomy to create a truly unique dining experience. The Lecture Room & Library holds three Michelin stars, while the other dining rooms offer equally impressive culinary delights.

The Ivy: A quintessentially British institution, The Ivy in Covent Garden is known for its classic menu and star-studded clientele. Its elegant yet relaxed atmosphere makes it a perfect spot for any occasion.

Luxury Shopping

For those who love to shop, London offers some of the best luxury shopping experiences in the world. From designer boutiques to high-end department stores, you'll find everything you need to indulge in a lavish lifestyle.

Harrods: Located in Knightsbridge, Harrods is one of the world's most famous department stores. It offers an extensive range of luxury goods, from designer fashion to gourmet food.

Bond Street: This prestigious shopping street in Mayfair is home to some of the world's most exclusive brands, including Chanel, Louis Vuitton, and Tiffany & Co. It's the perfect place to shop for high-end fashion, jewellery, and accessories.

Sloane Street: Located in Chelsea, Sloane Street is another top destination for luxury shopping. Here, you'll find flagship stores for brands like Gucci, Prada, and Versace.

Savile Row: For bespoke tailoring, Savile Row in Mayfair is the place to go. Renowned for its high-quality craftsmanship, it's the destination of choice for those seeking custom-made suits and attire.

Exclusive Clubs and Events

Socialising at exclusive clubs and attending high-profile events are integral parts of the millionaire lifestyle in London.

Private Members' Clubs:

The Arts Club: Located in Mayfair, this club is a haven for creatives and entrepreneurs, offering fine dining, live music, and a vibrant social scene.

Soho House: With several locations across London, Soho House is known for its chic ambiance and celebrity clientele. It's a great place to network and unwind.

High-Profile Events:

Royal Ascot: This prestigious horse racing event is a highlight of the British social calendar. It's known for its glamorous fashion, exclusive enclosures, and royal presence.

Chelsea Flower Show: Held annually in May, this event showcases the best in horticulture and garden design. It's a must-attend for gardening enthusiasts and socialites alike.

Wimbledon: The world's oldest tennis tournament, Wimbledon offers a blend of sport, tradition, and luxury. Secure a seat in the exclusive hospitality suites for a truly memorable experience.

Cultural and Leisure Activities

Living like a millionaire in London also means indulging in the city's rich cultural and leisure offerings. From world-class theatres to exclusive spas, there's no shortage of ways to enjoy your free time.

West End Theatre: London's West End is home to some of the best theatre productions in the world. For an opulent experience, book a private box at venues like the Royal Opera House or the Theatre Royal Drury Lane.

Art Galleries and Museums: Explore the city's renowned cultural institutions, such as the Tate Modern, the National Gallery, and the British

Museum. Many galleries offer exclusive events and private viewings for patrons.

Luxury Spas: Unwind and rejuvenate at one of London's top luxury spas. The Bulgari Spa in Knightsbridge, the Aman Spa at The Connaught, and the ESPA Life at Corinthia offer bespoke treatments in sumptuous settings.

Private Tours and Experiences: For a unique and personalised experience, consider booking private tours of historic landmarks, bespoke shopping experiences, or gourmet food tours.

High-End Transport

Getting around London in style is an essential part of the millionaire lifestyle. From luxury cars to private jets, there are numerous ways to travel in comfort and elegance.

Chauffeur Services: Companies like Addison Lee and Tristar Worldwide offer premium chauffeur services, providing luxury vehicles and professional drivers to ensure a comfortable and seamless journey.

Private Jets and Helicopters: For quick and convenient travel, consider chartering a private jet or helicopter. Companies like NetJets and London Helicopter Charters offer bespoke travel solutions for discerning clients.

Yachts and Boats: Explore London's waterways in style by chartering a luxury yacht or boat. Enjoy a private cruise along the Thames, complete with fine dining and breathtaking views of the city's landmarks.

Conclusion

Living like a millionaire in London is about more than just wealth; it's about experiencing the best that the city has to offer. From residing in prime neighbourhoods and dining at exclusive restaurants to indulging in luxury shopping and enjoying high-profile events, London provides endless opportunities for a lavish and fulfilling lifestyle.

Embrace the opulence, explore the possibilities, and make the most of your millionaire experience in one of the world's greatest cities.

MAINTAINING A BALANCED LIFE

Work-Life Balance

Achieving financial success in a bustling city like London often requires significant effort and dedication. However, it's essential to maintain a balance between work and personal life to ensure overall well-being and long-term happiness.

Set Boundaries: Establish clear boundaries between work and personal life. Designate specific times for work and stick to them, avoiding work-related tasks during personal time.

Prioritise Time Management: Use tools like calendars, planners, and time-tracking apps to manage your schedule effectively. Prioritise tasks based on importance and deadlines to ensure you allocate time for both work and leisure activities.

Learn to Say No: Overcommitting can lead to burnout. Assess your workload and be realistic about what you can handle. Politely decline additional tasks or projects that you cannot manage without compromising your well-being.

Schedule Downtime: Make time for relaxation and leisure activities. Whether it's reading a book, going for a walk, or spending time with family and friends, scheduling downtime helps you recharge and maintain balance.

Delegate When Possible: If you have a team or can afford to outsource certain tasks, delegate responsibilities to lighten your workload and focus on high-priority activities.

Stress Management

Managing stress is crucial for maintaining a balanced life and ensuring your physical and mental health.

Practice Mindfulness: Mindfulness techniques such as meditation, deep breathing exercises, and yoga can help reduce stress and improve focus. Incorporate these practices into your daily routine to stay calm and centred.

Stay Active: Regular physical activity is a powerful stress reliever. Aim for at least 30 minutes of exercise most days of the week, whether it's walking, running, cycling, or participating in a fitness class.

Get Adequate Sleep: Ensure you get enough sleep each night. Aim for 7-9 hours of quality sleep to support overall health and reduce stress.

Maintain a Healthy Diet: A balanced diet rich in fruits, vegetables, lean proteins, and whole grains can improve your energy levels and resilience to stress. Avoid excessive caffeine and sugar intake, which can contribute to anxiety and mood swings.

Seek Support: Don't hesitate to reach out to friends, family, or a mental health professional if you're feeling overwhelmed. Talking about your concerns can provide relief and perspective.

Social Connections

Building and maintaining strong social connections can enhance your quality of life and provide a support system during challenging times.

Stay Connected with Loved Ones: Regularly spend time with family and friends. Social interactions can boost your mood and provide emotional support.

Join Clubs and Groups: Participate in clubs, hobby groups, or community organisations that interest you. Engaging in shared activities can help you meet new people and build meaningful relationships.

Network Professionally: Attend industry events, conferences, and meetups to expand your professional network. Building connections in your field can provide support, advice, and potential opportunities.

Volunteer: Volunteering for causes you care about can provide a sense of purpose and fulfilment. It's also a great way to meet like-minded individuals and give back to the community.

Personal Growth and Fulfilment

Pursuing personal growth and fulfilment is essential for a balanced and satisfying life.

Set Personal Goals: In addition to financial and career goals, set personal development goals. These might include learning a new skill, travelling, or pursuing a hobby.

Embrace Lifelong Learning: Continuously seek opportunities to learn and grow. Take courses, attend workshops, read books, and stay curious about the world around you.

Celebrate Achievements: Acknowledge and celebrate your achievements, both big and small. Recognising your progress can boost your confidence and motivation.

Practice Gratitude: Regularly take time to reflect on and appreciate the positive aspects of your life. Keeping a gratitude journal can help you focus on the good and maintain a positive outlook.

Giving Back

Contributing to your community and helping others can enhance your sense of purpose and fulfilment.

Philanthropy: Consider donating to causes and organisations that are meaningful to you. Financial contributions can make a significant impact and support important work in your community.

Volunteer Work: Offer your time and skills to volunteer for local charities, non-profits, or community projects. Volunteering can provide personal satisfaction and a sense of connection to your community.

Mentorship: Share your knowledge and experience by mentoring others. Helping someone else succeed can be incredibly rewarding and contribute to your own growth and happiness.

Practical Tips for Maintaining Balance

Regularly Assess Your Balance: Periodically review your work-life balance and make adjustments as needed. Listen to your body and mind, and be proactive in addressing any imbalances.

Create a Balanced Routine: Develop a daily routine that includes time for work, exercise, relaxation, social activities, and personal growth. A well-rounded routine can help you manage your time and maintain balance.

Be Flexible: Life can be unpredictable, and flexibility is key to maintaining balance. Be open to adjusting your plans and priorities as circumstances change.

Seek Joy in Everyday Life: Find joy and satisfaction in everyday activities. Whether it's enjoying a cup of tea, spending time in nature, or practising a hobby, small moments of happiness contribute to overall well-being.

Prioritise Self-Care: Make self-care a priority. Taking care of your physical, emotional, and mental health is essential for maintaining balance and achieving long-term success.

Conclusion

Maintaining a balanced life is essential for achieving and sustaining financial success and overall well-being. By setting boundaries, managing stress, nurturing social connections, pursuing personal growth, and giving back to the community, you can create a fulfilling and harmonious life.

As you strive for wealth and success, remember that true prosperity encompasses not only financial achievements but also health, happiness, and a sense of purpose. Thank you for embarking on this journey with "A Londoner's Guide to Getting Rich." May your path to wealth be balanced, rewarding, and fulfilling.

WHO'S ALREADY WINNING?

London is home to some of the wealthiest individuals in the world, attracting billionaires from diverse industries such as finance, real estate, technology, and retail. This chapter delves into the lives and fortunes of some of the richest people in London, exploring their backgrounds, how they amassed their wealth, and their influence on the city.

Sir Jim Ratcliffe

Background: Sir Jim Ratcliffe is the founder and chairman of Ineos, a multinational chemicals company.

Wealth: With a net worth estimated at over £15 billion, Ratcliffe is one of the richest men in the UK.

Business Ventures: Ratcliffe's wealth comes from his majority stake in Ineos, which he built into a global powerhouse. The company has a diverse portfolio, including chemicals, oil and gas, automotive, and sports.

Lifestyle: Ratcliffe resides in Chelsea and is known for his interest in sports, particularly sailing and football. He owns OGC Nice, a French football club, and has made significant investments in British cycling.

Sir Leonard Blavatnik

Background: Sir Leonard Blavatnik is a Ukrainian-born British-American businessman, investor, and philanthropist.

Wealth: Blavatnik's net worth is estimated at over £20 billion, making him one of the wealthiest individuals in the UK.

Business Ventures: He founded Access Industries, a private industrial group with investments in natural resources, chemicals, media, and real estate. His acquisition of Warner Music Group significantly boosted his fortune.

Lifestyle: Blavatnik owns a lavish home in Kensington Palace Gardens, often referred to as "Billionaires' Row." He is a notable philanthropist, donating to various causes, including education, science, and the arts.

Sir James Dyson

Background: Sir James Dyson is a British inventor, industrial designer, and entrepreneur, best known for founding Dyson Ltd.

Wealth: Dyson's net worth is estimated at around £16 billion.

Business Ventures: Dyson revolutionised household appliances with his bagless vacuum cleaner. His company has since expanded into other innovative products, including hand dryers, fans, and hair dryers.

Lifestyle: Dyson owns multiple properties in the UK, including a grand estate in Gloucestershire. He is known for his investments in agricultural land and is a significant player in the UK's tech and innovation sectors.

David and Simon Reuben

Background: David and Simon Reuben are British businessmen and philanthropists.

Wealth: Their combined net worth is estimated at over £20 billion.

Business Ventures: The Reuben brothers made their fortune in metals trading and property investments. Their real estate portfolio includes prime London properties, such as Millbank Tower and the John Lewis Partnership headquarters.

Lifestyle: The Reuben brothers are known for their low profile but luxurious lifestyles. They are significant philanthropists, supporting numerous causes in education, healthcare, and the arts.

Alisher Usmanov

Background: Alisher Usmanov is a Russian-Uzbek businessman and oligarch.

Wealth: Usmanov's net worth is estimated at around £13 billion.

Business Ventures: Usmanov has interests in metals, mining, telecommunications, and media. He made significant investments in companies like Facebook and Alibaba, which contributed to his wealth.

Lifestyle: Usmanov owns Beechwood House in Hampstead and Sutton Place in Surrey. He is known for his art collection and philanthropy, particularly in sports and education.

Roman Abramovich

Background: Roman Abramovich is a Russian-Israeli billionaire, known for his ownership of Chelsea Football Club.

Wealth: Abramovich's net worth is estimated at around £9 billion.

Business Ventures: Abramovich amassed his fortune through investments in oil, steel, and aluminium industries. His acquisition of Chelsea FC transformed the club into one of the most successful in Europe.

Lifestyle: Abramovich resides in a luxurious mansion in Kensington and owns several other properties around the world. He is known for his extravagant lifestyle, including owning yachts, private jets, and a significant art collection.

Sir Philip Green

Background: Sir Philip Green is a British retail tycoon.
Wealth: Green's net worth is estimated at around £2 billion.

Business Ventures: Green made his fortune through his ownership of Arcadia Group, which included brands like Topshop, Burton, and Dorothy Perkins.

Lifestyle: Green owns a lavish home in Knightsbridge and is known for his luxurious lifestyle, including yachts, private jets, and high-profile parties.

Nassef Sawiris

Background: Nassef Sawiris is an Egyptian businessman and investor.

Wealth: Sawiris' net worth is estimated at around £6 billion.

Business Ventures: Sawiris is a scion of Egypt's wealthiest family and has significant investments in construction, chemicals, and technology. He owns stakes in companies like Adidas and Orascom Construction.

Lifestyle: Sawiris owns a home in London and is known for his philanthropic efforts, particularly in education and healthcare.

Conclusion

London is a magnet for some of the wealthiest individuals in the world, each contributing to the city's dynamic economy and cultural landscape.

From industrial magnates and technology innovators to retail tycoons and media moguls, these billionaires not only enjoy luxurious lifestyles but also significantly impact the industries and communities they engage with.

Understanding the backgrounds and ventures of these wealthy individuals provides insight into the diverse ways that fortunes can be built and maintained in one of the world's greatest cities.

NAVIGATING ECONOMIC CYCLES

Understanding Economic Cycles

Economic cycles, also known as business cycles, are fluctuations in economic activity over time. They consist of periods of expansion (growth) and contraction (recession). Understanding these cycles is crucial for making informed financial decisions and safeguarding your wealth.

Expansion: During expansion, the economy grows, characterized by increased employment, consumer spending, and business investment. This period typically sees rising asset prices, including stocks and property.

Peak: The peak marks the highest point of economic activity before a downturn begins. Indicators such as high consumer confidence, low unemployment, and rising inflation often signal an approaching peak.

Contraction: Contraction, or recession, occurs when economic activity declines. It is marked by falling employment, reduced consumer spending, and lower business investment. Asset prices often decrease during this period.

Trough: The trough is the lowest point of economic activity before recovery begins. It is characterized by economic stabilization and the start of a new expansion phase.

Strategies for Different Economic Phases
Adapting your financial strategies to the different phases of the economic cycle can help protect your wealth and take advantage of opportunities.

During Expansion:

Invest Aggressively: Take advantage of rising markets by investing in stocks, property, and other growth assets. Diversify your portfolio to spread risk.

Build an Emergency Fund: Use the period of prosperity to build a robust emergency fund. Aim for six to twelve months of living expenses to cover potential income disruptions.

Pay Down Debt: Take advantage of higher income levels to pay down high-interest debt, reducing your financial liabilities.

During Peak:

Reassess Investments: Review your investment portfolio and consider rebalancing to reduce exposure to overvalued assets. Shift some investments to safer, lower-risk options.

Increase Savings: Boost your savings rate to prepare for potential economic downturns. Consider keeping more cash on hand or in easily accessible accounts.

Lock in Rates: If you have variable-rate loans or mortgages, consider refinancing to lock in fixed rates before interest rates potentially rise.

During Contraction:

Preserve Capital: Focus on preserving your capital by shifting to safer investments like bonds, savings accounts, or low-risk funds. Avoid making high-risk investments during this period.

Cut Non-Essential Spending: Reduce discretionary spending and prioritize essential expenses. This will help you maintain financial stability during uncertain times.

Take Advantage of Opportunities: Look for undervalued assets, such as stocks or property, that may be available at lower prices. However, proceed cautiously and conduct thorough research.

During Trough:

Prepare for Recovery: Position yourself for the upcoming expansion by gradually increasing investments in growth assets. Consider investing in industries likely to benefit from the recovery.

Rebuild Savings: Continue to save and rebuild your emergency fund if it was depleted during the contraction phase.

Evaluate Career Opportunities: Economic recoveries often bring new job opportunities. Consider advancing your career or starting a business as the economy improves.

Diversification

Diversification is a key strategy for managing risk and navigating economic cycles. By spreading your investments across various asset classes, industries, and geographies, you can reduce the impact of economic downturns on your portfolio.

Asset Class Diversification: Invest in a mix of stocks, bonds, real estate, and alternative investments to balance risk and return.

Industry Diversification: Spread investments across different sectors, such as technology, healthcare, finance, and consumer goods, to mitigate sector-specific risks.

Geographic Diversification: Invest in both domestic and international markets to reduce the impact of regional economic downturns.

Staying Informed

Keeping informed about economic trends and indicators can help you make timely and informed financial decisions.

Monitor Economic Indicators: Keep an eye on key economic indicators such as GDP growth, unemployment rates, inflation, and interest rates. These indicators can provide insights into the current phase of the economic cycle.

Read Financial News: Stay updated with financial news from reputable sources. This will help you understand market trends and economic developments.

Consult Experts: Seek advice from financial advisors or economists who can provide professional insights and recommendations based on current economic conditions.

Practical Tips for Navigating Economic Cycles

Have a Long-Term Perspective: Economic cycles are natural and inevitable. Maintain a long-term perspective and avoid making hasty decisions based on short-term market fluctuations.

Maintain Flexibility: Be flexible with your financial plans and ready to adapt to changing economic conditions. Regularly review and adjust your strategies as needed.

Stay Calm During Volatility: Economic downturns can be stressful, but it's important to stay calm and avoid panic selling. Stick to your long-term plan and make decisions based on careful analysis.

Conclusion

Navigating economic cycles requires understanding the different phases and adapting your financial strategies accordingly. By diversifying your investments, staying informed, and maintaining a long-term perspective, you can protect your wealth and take advantage of opportunities in any economic climate.

The next chapter will explore the importance of continuous learning and personal development, providing strategies to enhance your skills, knowledge, and overall financial well-being.

CONTINUOUS LEARNING AND PERSONAL DEVELOPMENT

The Importance of Lifelong Learning

In today's fast-paced and ever-changing world, continuous learning and personal development are essential for maintaining a competitive edge and achieving long-term success. Embracing a mindset of lifelong learning helps you stay updated with industry trends, enhances your skills, and opens up new opportunities for personal and professional growth.

Adaptability: The ability to adapt to new situations and challenges is crucial. Continuous learning helps you stay agile and responsive to changes in the job market, technology, and industry trends.

Career Advancement: Ongoing education and skill development can lead to career progression, higher earning potential, and job satisfaction. Employers value individuals who demonstrate a commitment to learning and self-improvement.

Personal Fulfilment: Learning new skills and acquiring knowledge can be personally fulfilling and boost your confidence. It also provides a sense of achievement and motivation to pursue further growth.

Setting Learning Goals

To make the most of your continuous learning journey, it's essential to set clear and achievable learning goals. These goals will guide your efforts and keep you focused on your personal and professional development.

Identify Areas for Improvement: Assess your current skills and knowledge to identify areas where you need improvement. Consider seeking feedback from peers, mentors, or supervisors to gain insights.

Set SMART Goals: Ensure your learning goals are Specific, Measurable, Achievable, Relevant, and Time-bound. For example, "I want to complete an advanced Excel course within three months to improve my data analysis skills."

Create a Learning Plan: Develop a structured plan outlining the steps you need to take to achieve your goals. Include specific resources, timelines, and milestones to track your progress.

Leveraging Online Learning Platforms

Online learning platforms offer a convenient and flexible way to acquire new skills and knowledge. These platforms provide access to a wide range of courses, tutorials, and resources from the comfort of your home.

Coursera: Coursera offers courses from top universities and institutions, covering various subjects, including business, technology, and personal development. Many courses offer certificates upon completion.

Udemy: Udemy provides a vast library of courses on diverse topics, often created by industry professionals. Courses are usually affordable, and you can learn at your own pace.

edX: Similar to Coursera, edX offers courses from renowned universities and institutions. It covers a broad range of subjects, and many courses are free to audit.

LinkedIn Learning: LinkedIn Learning offers professional development courses, focusing on skills such as leadership, project management, and technical skills. The platform also integrates with your LinkedIn profile.

Khan Academy: Khan Academy provides free educational resources on various subjects, including mathematics, science, and finance. It's an excellent resource for foundational learning.

Developing Soft Skills

In addition to technical skills, soft skills are crucial for personal and professional success. These skills enhance your ability to work effectively with others and adapt to different environments.

Communication: Effective communication skills are essential for conveying ideas, building relationships, and resolving conflicts. Practice active listening, clear articulation, and empathetic responses.

Leadership: Strong leadership skills enable you to inspire and guide others. Focus on developing skills such as decision-making, delegation, and team motivation.

Emotional Intelligence: Emotional intelligence involves understanding and managing your emotions and those of others. It helps build strong interpersonal relationships and enhances teamwork.

Problem-Solving: The ability to analyse situations, identify problems, and develop solutions is highly valued in any field. Practice critical thinking and creative problem-solving techniques.

Time Management: Effective time management skills help you prioritise tasks, meet deadlines, and maintain a healthy work-life balance. Use tools like planners, calendars, and productivity apps to stay organised.

Pursuing Certifications and Qualifications

Obtaining certifications and qualifications can validate your skills and knowledge, making you more attractive to employers and clients.

Professional Certifications: Many industries offer certifications that demonstrate your expertise in specific areas. Examples include PMP (Project Management Professional) for project management, CFA (Chartered Financial Analyst) for finance, and CISSP (Certified Information Systems Security Professional) for cybersecurity.

Academic Qualifications: Consider pursuing higher education degrees, such as a master's degree or MBA, to deepen your knowledge and enhance your credentials.

Specialised Training: Enrol in specialised training programs that focus on specific skills or technologies relevant to your field. These programs often provide hands-on experience and practical knowledge.

Networking and Knowledge Sharing

Engaging with peers and industry professionals can enhance your learning experience and provide valuable insights.

Join Professional Associations: Becoming a member of professional associations allows you to network with industry experts, attend events, and access exclusive resources.

Attend Conferences and Workshops: Participate in conferences, workshops, and seminars to stay updated with industry trends and expand your professional network.

Engage in Online Communities: Join online forums, discussion groups, and social media communities related to your field. Share knowledge, ask questions, and learn from others' experiences.

Mentorship: Seek out mentors who can provide guidance, advice, and support. Mentors can offer valuable perspectives based on their own experiences and help you navigate your career path.

Practical Tips for Continuous Learning

Allocate Time for Learning: Dedicate regular time for learning and personal development. Schedule study sessions, set aside time for reading, and participate in relevant activities.

Stay Curious: Cultivate a curious mindset and a passion for learning. Embrace new challenges and seek opportunities to expand your knowledge.

Reflect on Your Progress: Periodically review your learning goals and assess your progress. Reflecting on your achievements and areas for improvement can help you stay motivated and focused.

Stay Open to Feedback: Embrace feedback from peers, mentors, and supervisors. Constructive feedback can provide valuable insights and help you improve continuously.

Apply What You Learn: Put your new skills and knowledge into practice. Applying what you learn reinforces your understanding and demonstrates your capabilities to others.

Conclusion

Continuous learning and personal development are vital for achieving long-term success and fulfilment. By setting clear learning goals, leveraging online learning platforms, developing soft skills, pursuing certifications, and engaging with your professional network, you can enhance your skills, stay competitive, and open up new opportunities.

Embrace a mindset of lifelong learning, and remember that personal growth is an ongoing journey. The next chapter will explore how to create a sustainable and meaningful life by integrating financial success with purpose and fulfilment.

CONCLUSION

THE END

Please leave a review :)

ABOUT THE AUTHOR

Genevieve Velzian

Genevieve Velzian is a successful digital nomad and entrepreneur, who employs many of the strategies detailed in this book. She works remotely and has been fortunate enough to explore much of the world in the last 2 years - next up is China!

www.ingramcontent.com/pod-product-compliance
Lightning Source LLC
Chambersburg PA
CBHW031433210526
45464CB00005B/2176